O Lucky Day

Poems

Praise for *O Lucky Day* by Patricia Clark

O Lucky Day by Patricia Clark makes a reader feel luckier in every possible way. The potent pacing of these poems, their gracious attention to sound and flow, and deeply grounded considerations—woods, birds, plants, beloved people—improve the spirit right away. Life feels richer, more available somehow—nearer and dearer in a traumatic time of too many conflicts. We need this wisdom, cheer, and truthful gaze.

—Naomi Shihab Nye, author of *Grace Notes: Poems about Families*

In the poems of Patricia Clark's fine new book, *O Lucky Day*, the title's enthusiasm is tempered by the knowledge of losses and inflected with subtle surprises of survival. There's a buoyant yet quiet sense of wonder rippling through these poems, "relishing the juice" of living, even as the speaker prepares for what comes next: "how I train myself // to disappear, into . . . / the viburnum just about to flower." Praise for a long marriage, the loss of friends and beloveds, the self-awareness of both vitality and mortality—these comprise the clarifying paradox of *O Lucky Day*. Particularly moving are elegies for her father and for her mentor, Stanley Plumly, but all along it's the natural world that provides Clark with her richest variety of beauty, fragility, and obstinate song.

—David Baker, author of *Whale Fall and Swift:*
New & Selected Poems

From the first poem "Oxygen" and throughout the book, these contemplative poems will breathe new life into your soul. Patricia Clark's poems are rich with metaphors and filled with fresh ways of looking at the everyday. Her poem "What My Father Wished For" shares an honest and moving expression of the meaning of life near the end. The father states, "I've had everything in this life I could have wanted." Beautiful! I highly recommend this new collection by one of Michigan's finest and best known poets.

—M.L. Liebler, author of *Underneath My American Face:*
Five Decades of Selected Poetry

Also by Patricia Clark

North of Wondering (1999, reprinted 2003)

My Father on a Bicycle (2005)

She Walks into the Sea (2009)

Sunday Rising (2013)

The Canopy (2017)

Self-Portrait with a Million Dollars (2020)

O Lucky Day

Poems

Patricia Clark

MADVILLE
PUBLISHING

LAKE DALLAS, TEXAS

Requests for permission to reprint or reuse material
from this work should be sent to:

Permissions
Madville Publishing
PO Box 358
Lake Dallas, TX 75065

Cover Design: Kimberly Davis
Cover Art: *Still Life with Clementine*,
Jos Van Riswick, josvanriswick.com
Author Photo: Grand Valley State University

ISBN: 978-1-963695-07-6 paperback
978-1-963695-08-3 ebook
Library of Congress Control Number: 2024939288

for Stanley Krohmer, my love,
my painter, my rock, my muse

Contents

III.

Love is just the retaliation of light.

It is so profligate, you know,
so rich with rush.

—Alice Fulton

Oxygen: Letter to My Husband After a Quarrel

I'm sorry my mother got a blood clot in her lung
       and couldn't come with me to Italy,

and I'm sorry I never went fishing with my father—
       the fly rod he gave me gathers dust.

It turns out she never got to use her passport,
       no stamp for Italy or Greece.

The steelhead I might have caught
       with my father's instructions still lie

silver on the pebbly riverbed of the Satsop
       or the Stillaguamish.

I'm sorry about the dams, how they prevent
       the return of fish to spawn.

And the owls nesting out there in the Olympic
       Forest: I regret the grand trees

felled for home construction. I would protect
       the rain forest and owl habitat.

I'm sorry I'm bossy and can't sit
       still. You might have it right

sit and meditate. If I've hurt you,
       I'm sorry. In my seventieth year,

I vow to lounge a bit more, to loaf
       and to ponder.

I wanted to tell you that fear of death
       poked its nose into my neck

this morning, maybe because that show
       Still Game had Vincent

facing a life with his second leg
        cut off—his friends

trying to help, faking a death to get
        insurance money so he could fly

to Switzerland to save his leg.
        Isn't intimacy always about

circulation? Blood flow means
        oxygen, oxygen means life,

and I'm not just talking arteries, veins,
        blood but the whole mind-body

connection. You and me, my love, yin
        and some yang, some oil, some

water. If I keep meditating to get it
        right, fly rod in hand,

the fish are going to bite. I won't bring
        a steelhead home. They're a gift: catch

and release, kiddo. I'm trying to learn how.

I.

Forest Bathing

Each button undone,
        each tooth of a zipper
                gapped to let pants,

jacket fall open,
        each strap and hem
                of a top, blouse, shirt

says O skin, you have
        wanted this so much—to lie
                down, meadow grass

tickling, a see-through green, too early
        for mosquitoes (you hope),
                to have nothing

between you and petal, tendril,
        bundle of last year's
                milkweed packed, filament

upon filament in the pod, poised
        for release to scatter like bird-
                song, each thread carrying

a seed like a word on wind
        though not a syllable uttered,
                this splash in

what isn't liquid but spills out
        nevertheless—drift of grass blade,
                petals, blossom, leaf.

Juneberry Leaves as Gold Coins

It's October when you notice, when you walk out
        and touch its leaves.

Your peace was broken, then healed, then
        transformed.

You can't stay the same. And yet.

Later came the Japanese maple
        called *bloodgood.*
Mulch surrounded the trunk—a wide necklace of chips.

The year of allium, of the desire for a spring
        to end so much ruined by dark.

It's called commerce when you exchange,
        when you spend. This for a tree: delivered,
planted, two men with a Bobcat.

This much for four yards of mulch.

The furrows in the bark, or the smoothness,
        tell the tale. Shagbark,
        white oak, sycamore.

They all lose and come back. There's no
        sign of struggle—except the sycamore.

He said I wish you liked to be held.
        They stood under an unyielding sky, no
        sign of the space station.

I do, she said.

Sea Urchin

Hokusai's fisherman bends in half
                    on the tip
          of a promontory,

a jacket, short pants, a grass skirt
                    over the pants,
          no hat, tall socks

with shoes—though I'm fearful he'll slip
                    where below
          waves snarl and spit.

He's pulling in at least four lines, heavy
                    with fish,
          one has to hope—

and he's not alone. Nearby crouches a bearded man
                    down on his haunches
          also holding lines.

Yes, this land's rocky, but the outcrop looks
                    fragile enough
          to break off,

soft ground with wet sod crumbling
                    to pitch him in,
if not both of them. Once,

we wandered far down Agate & Crescent Beach,
                    stooping at
   tidepools, turning over rocks

to find small gray crabs and touch
                    anemones, fascinated
          by their pulse, heedless of tides.

By the time we looked up, our path back
                    was swallowed,
          water crashing in, spraying foam,

3

and only through luck did we find
                    a cut
        in the bluff where a path

snaked down—we clambered up with sea-
                    salt biting
        at our heels. That was the day

later on, we hauled in a creature of the deep
                            we didn't know,
            a purple spiny mound large

as a cabbage we brought to the park ranger
                        in a bucket—
        sea urchin, he said mildly.

My father and his father, me and who else?
                    —my brother Dan?—
        last seen on that rock-tumbled shore.

It was a fearsome beautiful creation—
            those spines dripping
        with brine, waving—I hope we let it go.

The Wind Phone

In the wrecked landscape
of Fukushima

a white telephone booth
shines

with many panes of glass
in the hinged door

and a man steps in
dials the cell number

of his wife's phone,
of course unanswering—

she was swept away
in the tsunami,

a photo in the paper
shows her sitting outside

on a blanket, knees
up, rocking back in laughter.

I pick up the black
receiver, still warm

from his hand, dialing
my sister's number I used

to know by heart.
No answer from the sea

or her, just the whirling sound
of blood pounding in my ear.

Poem Beginning with a Line from Adam Zagajewski

But the kingdom of the dead may be right here
And unrecognized. By *here* she must mean
Both garden and house, clothes closet, pantry,
Circle of mulch around the Japanese maple,
Coconut mat laid at the gingko's feet.
That's what she believed after they left,
Her parents, the day she used the word
Orphan with a friend drinking chardonnay,
her face tightening, shadowed, who said,
"No, you can't be one—that's for kids
Without parents." Then why the persistent
Ache and a blank space on her mind's horizon
Where they'd stood like poplars? She couldn't
Say oaks, their figures were more slender, flexible
In stiff wind. Look it up: bereaved is the root.

Fathering

From our house I feel the pull
that calendar and clock make—a friend

> to meet for lunch. The two penned hounds next door
> go crazy—seeing what I see: a small shaggy deer
> out back, heading west through russet leaves, stepping
> and bending, chewing as it goes on the last green
> of mulberry or Virginia creeper vine.

In this last year, my friend lost her mother;
her father never writes from France
or calls. She says he never remembered her
birthday once, as a child or now. What is

> a father for? My own's been gone nearly
> thirty years—how he gave me money,
> twice, when I was in a jam, taught me how to park
> parallel in a spot, showed how a grown man can play

touch football or a board game, laughing
like a child. Swimming at American Lake,
holding me in his arms. I still see the light
that afternoon and pebbles shining through water—

> how he scooped two of us from a dark pool.

Because What We Do Lives On

This is not my gruff grandfather. Not his hat
or his cigar boxes, still fragrant. This is what she said
late in his life, going over to his small house
with frozen pipes. His grown son crawled under the house
with a hairdryer, an extension cord, cobwebs
and spiders everywhere in his hair, caught
on his sleeves. *What's he doing now?* the voice
was not her husband's. *Why is he taking so
fucking long?* When they were first married, she worked
to welcome these people into her life, her children's
lives. Christmas morning breakfast with cinnamon
rolls and gifts. Years of gifts for the kids: a plastic comb,
a pleated plastic rain bonnet, a card of bobby pins.
She sat in the kitchen with him, the table
with a jar of bacon fat next to the pepper and salt.
If you ever speak to him like that again, she
breathed, *we won't be back.* My mother,
gone some nineteen years but living on
with her iron fierceness. *If you ever!*
And my grandfather sat silent, holding his
hat in his hands, stopping his tongue. This
is not his voice, his unshaven cheek, that
kitchen and its worn linoleum floor.

Silver-Tipped Japanese Grass

"Please do not worry," they said.

"Let the weight
bend you over. There will be a time
for rising. Not today."

I vowed to watch the grasses, their pale
wheat-colored froth of seed heads
through winter days ahead,

noticing how they held on despite
snow and ice, to celebrate

in wind and rain how they flexed,
were jostled and battered, but stayed.
An ice storm bent them flat.

When ice melts, stems and seed heads rising
again, I let wind touch my cheek.
My skin tender, it yields.

Give Me a Face to Cover My Face

I've looked at myself too long.

Thin lips, one eyebrow dented in,
almost hairless, and those gray pools

underneath my eyes. I could tell you
the history of the lines around my mouth,

the estuaries at corners of my eyes.
Right in the center of my face,

the prow of my nose pushing its way
into the day's new hours. If not

entirely straight, it wears its charms,
detecting saltwater from miles off,

burnt toast at twenty feet. Years
ago, finding Modigliani's portraits,

I relaxed into my own—falling in love
with his models' dark hair, eyes

like coal, wearing berets and peach
or aubergine scarves, or sometimes

they were swan-necked nudes, a blush of ruddy shyness
on their cheeks. Embracing

asymmetry, I could love them all more
than me, over time. If we aren't

the surfaces of ourselves—who is it
lurking beneath, hoping to sneak out—

a hermit crab pulling its shell
behind it on damp sand, scrawling

a mark in some illegible obscure
calligraphy, tugging and taking on

the shell's weight, there on a neap
tide night, waves glinting at the edge.

Quarentena

I gather the eight
days in Venice
into a garland
to wrap around my wrist
or maybe as a braid
to weave into
my hair. I pierce
gathered buds with
needle and thread,
making a blossom row,
yellow, red, white,
and pink, repeat,
repeat. It takes
an ego to make
of captivity a song.
I lean out on my
balcony, yellow wall
and white balustrade—
where I bow once
to the Giardini Reali—
lush garden below me
whose pergola I came
to love—and second
to the Isola di San
Giorgio Maggiore—
thank you for your steady
Easter bells, for your
upright standing in full
moonlight and for
allowing me to bend
and cry a little for what's
always lost no matter
how we crack open
our mouths, wetting our
lips, trying to send a word
or two out on our
singular breath.

Sailor

Never to be erased, now, how a word
comes back when I see a riffle on the face
of the river, *fetch*.

Never the imperative said to a dog,
we never had a dog together, never the kids
who waited in shadow.

And I suppose never a proper goodbye.
When was it I Googled his name? There
it was, an obituary, end.

Sailboat, and his dream, never to come:
a catamaran, a voyage to New Zealand.
The vocabulary of boats—

I thank him now for that, a fetch
may indicate weather, or maybe a shoal
to steer away from.

Mainsail and jib, rudder, lines, and keel.
Coming about, the danger of the boom.
And the telltale, high

on the mast. What we tried, five years,
was not to be. Never a regret, but words stay.
Boat without a name. Fetch.

Astronomy "In Perfect Silence"

in memoriam Professor George Wallerstein

A million-petalled flower of being there, Seattle,
    beside Bagley Hall in a time long ago,
  can you see the magic in the water,
    Drumheller Fountain, Lake Washington, Mt. Rainier
  even as students rush inside to class? Never
forget what enthusiasm for a subject can do:

gone the professor's name but not these lessons—
    how Intro to Astronomy never left me.
  Important to look up at the stars, each day,
    just to remember our insignificance. All term,
  know that we're mere specks. Keep reading,
learning about blue dwarfs, red giants, binary stars, our silver

moon and other celestial bodies, constellations, comets,
    nebulae, all the ways scientists study
  our universe from a distance. Where is Earth's
    place if everything's streaming away?
  Quasars and quarks—these aren't the only
rich mysteries. There's more. Dark matter, black holes,

serious topics still to be figured out. In the book, star charts,
    timely as always. I step out with one, frigid January,
  under a brilliant sky. Auriga, Capella, Pleiades, and there's
Venus rising. A skyscape admired each time.
  Walt Whitman was right: somehow to balance
excitement with knowledge. Seeing night skies again:

    yearly, monthly, daily—gazing overhead, still awed,
zealous, "I look'd up in perfect silence at the stars."

Soldier Boy

You can come to me, Robert, one last time, late morning
        or at dusk, before I close the door, come to me
    with the sweat of your uniform, smell of cigarettes,
        with a duffel bag, guitar case, tunes ready
    to sing to me and all the ghosts gathered near us
        that summer fifty years ago.
      The words of Arlo Guthrie, Bob Dylan,
    memories of buddies you left behind, with names
      like in the movies—Rat, Alabama, Surf.

Bring anything you'd like, photos from Vietnam,
you and buddies posing by a tank or near a tent,
bring the names of Cambodia and Saigon, names
    carrying a smell of gasoline and forest leaves, the sound
    of choppers and someone crying.

I'd like to see what you'd share, what you'd
        hide—a photo of your home in Silver Springs,
    your father's construction business, your mother's
      tired face, and Susan, your only sibling.
    She holds a clutch of colored pens.

I'll bring saltwater air from Tacoma out west,
        beach stones from Browns Point, a madrona
    leaf and a piece of sienna crackling bark from the trunk.
      I'll bring a young girl's packet of letters
    saved from her pen pal soldier, come to Fort
      Lewis to take her to dinner.

I won't forget how it all spun out, the sleepy
        bear on the motel sign near U Village,
    the shadow of the 45th Street viaduct, rumble
      of cars, the French wine you bought along
    with gold-rimmed glasses, a corkscrew.
      I had read *A Farewell to Arms*, I'd never had wine.
    When you said "Marry me," my body thrilled to yes.

I'm finally admitting the tale of my two trips
        east, staying with you and your family.

Soon your mother wanted our wedding guest list.
        Nightly you talked hours on the phone,
soft words, with another Patricia in the hospital
having an abortion. Isn't it time, at last,
to come clean on what the story was?

Say again, as you did, she meant nothing.

Tell that to my cracked heart. My family had opposed you—
        how could I say, now, they'd been right
all along. Not to be, a wedding, children to join
        my sisters' kids. That spring, as Kent State headlined
the news, students shot dead, I could finally
        bend and wail. My college freshman year.

Come toward me with your slick email years later,
        "When I say love, I mean forever." This
        is my garden, another self of mine you've
never imagined or known: cosmos, zinnia, feathery
        astilbe in spires of red. How could I be lured
into believing you again? It beggars
        my mind. From my bedroom window I hear
around 4 a.m. a train whistle heading
        out of town, engine tugging memory-slow.

Many a summer night here finds us seated under oaks
        by a fire, my husband, me, a handful
of friends. Once it's lit, we keep it burning as long
        as we can, someone getting up, each time, to turn
a log or poke at coals. If we tell stories, woodsmoke wreathing us,
        they're often for laughs, never about lost moments
        in a buried past. None of these folks
know your name, count on it, and Vietnam's
        an ancient war, also lost.

Inscape, with Birdsong

I learned the filament holding up the anther
     and how, with daylilies, it was good
          to clip off the pollen-stuck ends—

before my white sleeve or the damask tablecloth.
     I learned the placement of tableware,
          goblets and glasses—water, wine.

I didn't learn the weight of crystal, the price
     of accumulation. I learned, instead,
          to dawdle and dream, the art of

lifting myself to the noble place of green serenity
     where thought matured along with reflection.
          The singer high in the oak

surprised me with its melody. Not, after all,
     the oriole. A look through binoculars
          brought a robin into view, full-

throated, rust-red breast feathers.
     Padded bench, a cold drink, respite
          from weeding wild violets,

how specks of starts, green-heart small
     came up among gravel in the path,
          then drifted into the grass.

I learned some lore at a time, not
     everything at once, the robin's elegy,
          then the Baltimore oricle, arrow-orange,

shooting past, high, secretive, into a cottonwood.

I Consider Pruning the Magnolia Tree and Instead Take a Nap

A fall morning of exquisite cool air,
crystalline light—

I clean off the pruning shears
           with soap and water,

listening to a crow exclaim it sees a deer,

lifting down the wooden ladder,
         bearing it sideways into
             the front yard,

setting it up under a branch, testing soft
         ground to see how far
            it'll sink in.

Will I tip over? Am I safe?
         I sit for a minute on the front stoop,

my thumb picking up a beat
           in the artery of my neck
        where I rest my hand.

The Greek philosopher Pythagoras
         conceived of the metempsychosis

of souls—each departing body giving free
        rein for its soul to enter
           another body.

O to be a winged thing with hollow bones—
        free of ladders, pruning, falls.

Rose-breasted grosbeak, goldfinch, crow.
        Come out with me, love—and hold the ladder.

Bird migration south has already begun.

After My Husband Tries His New Electric Shaver

He comes to report to me
and once again thank me
for a Christmas gift wrapped
in red in the waning days
of a sour year, and I don't
tell him I've already seen
quarter-inch dark bits
of his beard on the sink's
bowl. I'm trying to learn
why repeating the small
failings of one's spouse
right before undressing
doesn't bring happiness.
He has remembered to
tuck in the sheet at
the bottom corner, to fluff
up my night-flattened
pillow—so I don't
bring up belly fat,
either his or mine,
my plan for more
veggies in our diet,
or how I wish
he'd walk with me
along the river, some
late afternoon of fading
gray light similar to
this January one.
In spite of my sore
shoulder, his newly
replaced right hip,
we roll together all
skin, touch, warmth
and I praise the chance
of it, our continued
eagerness, this third
day of a new year
and I look up to see
his face above me,

sun of my moon, skin
newly buzzed clean
and pink, my lips
mouthing under breath
lucky, O lucky day.

Passing Royalty: *Una Sfilata di Due*

I'm sorry I didn't comprehend sooner how threatening
       I could be, testing positive.

Mi dispiace for condemning a hotel clerk and a pharmacist,
       the latter who said he could call *la polizia.*

Non mi dispiace for liking the small town
       near the Venice airport—

Tessera, a little piece of the big mosaic that was
       Italy that year, where I learned to say *mille grazie.*

I'm sorry for the missed Fortuny Museum, a chartreuse scarf
       I would have bought, straight out

of Proust, and *Mi dispiace ancora* for no
       gondola ride, no Guggenheim Museum,

though I'd paid for tickets. I'm not sorry Easter
       was a balcony tolling

with many near and distant bells, a view across the lagoon
       to Isola di San Giorgio Maggiore and a full

moon. I'm not sorry for escaping in my mind
       with Henry James and Joseph Brodsky,

O watery city that is Venice, flooded or not, where
       we might have walked as boon companions.

I'm sorry my husband and I didn't explore the *Dorsoduro,*
       fin of the fish, or is it *high ridge*? The roofline

figurines nearby seemed to mock me. Some wore helmets or
       hats, tools in hand. I'm not sorry for the airport shuttle, thirty-five

euro to test negative, both of us crying. I'm sorry for all
       the traffic swooshing by, but I'm not sorry

for the gum wrapper shining like silver, a soda can
    glinting in sun, and for stout weeds coming up

purple and blue in a ditch, proclaiming the two of us
    as passing royalty, sure we'd be escorted, wrinkled clothes or

not, dust, masks and all, onto a plane by angels. My last
    glimpse of Tessera, there was a black cat crouching

in a field, following a butterfly's orange path,
    spectacular, ordinary, the afternoon before

    we lifted off.

Each Day I Undress

a clementine, using my small green
　　　ceramic knife, a ritual

the morning needs to be complete—
　　　I sit and look out, light

a candle against darkness and despair,
　　　peel off the thick pebbly skin

to get down to fruit. Then pulling apart
　　　sections, discarding the pith

or any stringy bits, I slowly place
　　　each wedge in my mouth.

I become a tongue, a being that tastes—
　　　relishing the juice, feeling thin

membranes yield. For those few
　　　minutes I think of nothing,

inhabiting tastebuds and mouth.
　　　It's how I train myself

to disappear, into the shagbark
　　　hickory, the scarred maple,

the viburnum just about to flower.
　　　In the moment, I'm inside one

of its buds, branch tip quivering,
　　　a tight knot of white and red,

knuckle size, a coiled energy about
　　　to burst into petalled pale

balls, most likely tomorrow—wafting their scent
　　　toward our bedroom windows

that I've left carelessly open, letting
　　　each particle of scent in.

Portrait of My Lover as a Promenade Along the Sea

Imagine concrete, and then,
in other places, ancient stone.
Duck under the rope, please,
to begin the way.

In some places, steep
stairs. Other places level
with a secure handrail.
Then, sheer
cliff face down to wave-crashed
rocks, spray.

Someone stood out there, fishing.
Extreme danger of the stance.
Isn't that how it is, O sweet,
taking our intimate risks?

Here, this breath.
Here, the outstretched hand.

Char

for Nathan, Joel, and Alison

On a rooftop downtown at the edge
of the building   where they've planted succulents
stands a horse   blackened by fire
called *Char* by its maker   Deborah Butterfield.
The artist scoured   a smoky ravaged forest
in California, picking up   branches, limbs,
burnt saplings, then brought   these to her studio
where she fashioned them   into the shape of a horse.
During the process, taking weeks,   Butterfield often dreams
of horses. This one   grazing in a meadow
where red-tipped grass   waved against its belly, seeds
catching in its long tail.   Horse has become the artist's
mirror self, a dream   figure made manifest.
After the studio, a foundry,   a way to cast
wood into metal,   finally pouring
bronze for the final sculpture.   The workers made marks
in metal to resemble wood,   adding a patina black
as night sky.   *Char* looks east into clouds
above our city,   ignoring for past weeks
the haze from Canada wildfires,   not pricking
its ears in terror   or flipping its tail.
Char is more skeleton than   mass, negative space
allowing us to glimpse what's been ruined and where
we stand, on the edge,   barely able to breathe.

Love Poem to a Red Fox

To your black-stockinged feet as you trot west.

To your bushy tail streaming behind you like a flame.

To whatever brings you near, plentiful squirrels and voles hiding
       in leaf litter. Woe unto them!

To your long muzzle, whiskers, white tip on your tail.

To the insouciant way you walk along a fallen tree, balancing,
       then jumping down.

To the way you bring me out of myself into your wild
       alertness, ears perked.

To the thick healthy fur keeping you warm.

To your hurrying by, as though late for a meeting,
       on a mission I cannot know.

To the musky scent you leave as you pass, one to drive
       the neighborhood dogs wild, howling.

To your scat with a tapered tail with embedded bits of mouse,
       rabbit, berries, or insects, bird feathers too.

To the demarcation you establish, the wild vs. the tame,
       the ordinary, and mundane: no wonder you intrigue me.

To your feet and a ridge of callus on the interdigital pad, says the field guide.

To your den I'll never find, fallen log, den you've dug out
       with an entrance marked by small bones. How many feasts?

To your habitat and range, to your trotting stride and trotting gait,
       thirty-two inches or more.

To whatever fills you, also to your dreams, do you twitch
       and shake, feet running in dreams like our dog? I see you
       in moonlight, glimmer-light.

To the chance of you, risk of you, joy of you red against the snow.

II.

Wrack Line

All I learned is what I love.
—Theodore Roethke

1.

If you go down to walk
beside the Grand River, do you
see it?

What's cast up, branches, twigs, a 2x4,
a plastic length of dental floss,
a wedge of Styrofoam, a shell or two—
here's what high water left:
all in a straight line, not ruler straight but
arranged, piled
ephemeral art from high water.

How water casts out what it can't use, as though to say, "You
take this!" Your wish: for other things to be cast
out, the chemicals dumped, wastewater
from fields and lawns, runoff phosphates, PFAS, oils, and grease
harmful to living things.
"Here, take this!"

2.

Everywhere it laps in, touches land, the lake-
water makes wetlands, especially waters blown by wind,
steady easterlies, the shore soaked, swales

in soft ground where deer step, make trails, and every spring
warblers fly in, find a marsh, early May, without fail,
groups of birds, tired, sometimes in a flock so large

they show up on radar. Imagine all these, drawn
by water, and juneberry, dogwood budding out when
insects hatch, in sequence. Later, Joe Pye weed

waves its large flat clusters, spotted stems,
food for butterflies, hummingbirds. Nearby, milkweed
that will leave its gray pods clacking in wind.

3.

The imp of the divine lives along the river,
democratic, among the tumbled chunks
of concrete, trees broken in half by last year's
storm, the asphalt path made smooth so the blind

can walk there and veterans from the Home
nearby. Why do you linger? To watch
the lovers bend to kiss, to see how wind
frets the water, to idle away an hour or two.

4.

Along the Rogue River in Rockford, Michigan
a company hires workers to tan leather, shaping
it into shoes. It's a business of vats and liquid, soaking,
waiting, turning, draining, drying, taking time.
Beamhouse and tanyard, first stage, second
stage. How did it work? Wooden vats, trenches.
Before rules on the environment. Did workers ever
object or quit? One man slams his hat down.
"I don't think we should pour this stuff
into the river. It stinks."

5.

Changed its name in the 1950s from Wolverine to Wolverine Worldwide,
    to show its scope.

Made by 3M in 1952: Scotchgard. To coat and repel water and dirt.

Debuted in 1958: their famous Hush Puppies and soon 1 in 10 adults
    claimed to have a pair.

They warned Wolverine Worldwide, in 1999, that the coating had dangers.

Still, the dumping went on, scraps of leather and discarded soles thrown as "fill"
        along House Street, along Rum Creek.

Wolverine said they didn't know, didn't know: vinyl chloride,
        trichloroethylene, mercury, chromium, and lead.

One of the attorneys asked, "Would you live downriver, allow your kids
        to play in or drink that water? What if your house relied on a well?"

6.

You never had a chance
                    to speak, pressed under and down
      by weight of water.

7.

Because living near the airport runway's end,
           they got used to the racket of jet engines,
because the planes came in low, flaps down,
because they were travelers, to the East, to Europe,
because they liked imagining the passengers,
           belted in, leaning back with closed eyes,
because they too dreamed of Paris, New York, Rome,
because one morning Nancy E. went out walking Bella
           and found cream-colored slime along the creek,
because de-icing the silver birds in winter was needed,
because propylene glycol starts off pink,
because airport officials said they had reduced
           the number of gallons from 80,000 gallons to 6,000,
because it was organic de-icing liquid,
because the amphibians had birth defects,
because the peepers didn't start up in spring,
because no amount of runoff was safe, because,
           think: would you pour this into water?

8.

Off the main path, I veer off asphalt
and walk closer to the river,

avoiding dogs with my dog.

It looks arranged by an artist
of the ephemeral, perhaps Andy Goldsworthy—

sticks, twigs, branches, leaves, eel grass.

A 6-inch-wide heap of what's been
cast up by high water, coughed out.

Not accidental, thus here to speak to me.

Above in trees, still bare, red-winged
blackbirds make their cries—*first, here.*

Mate seeking, nest building, harbingers.

We kick along, the black and white dog all nose,
ecstatic, nostrils and muzzle flaring, vibrating.

Her sensory attention astonishes me

as I count lockdown months, lament,
worry, fret—finally yielding to what I see,

admire—nature insistently pointing to spring.
The warblers back, and singing, right on schedule,

and Baltimore orioles, high in the canopy, their melodic
songs, yes, here, here, not going anywhere,

and back, swaying in the high branches, leaves
about to unfurl.

III.

When the Great Poet Is Gone from the Earth

for Stanley Plumly

Of course this world went on, and the election
was won but then there was trouble, a wild
insurrection, of which I imagine he'd have been upset.
And I learned that the singer in our trees
is named the great crested flycatcher, with moves
in the tall oaks exactly like the bird guide
describes, but more of a yeep than a song.
Now the season ended in leaf-fall,
blazing, as it always does, so much mowing,
then the green tractor stowed until spring.

When the great poet is gone you work
to remember his words, not coming up
with many, "Hey, kiddo!" are two words.
Blowing across the mouth of a bottle, moo,
words from a poem. And the city painted bike
lanes and the corner power boxes in wild
colorful graphics. They started mapping
the canopy, asking for citizen input.
Sales of his books didn't go up.

At the AWP conference where he was missed
by some, the young couldn't come up
with his name, and we strolled the book
exhibit endlessly, hoping to catch him
or a glimpse of his magnificent hair,
and at breakfast he was still absent,
never there in his cashmere jacket or greeting
old students or older lovers. His handwriting
didn't come in the mail though I uncovered
an old postcard, a few words still illegible.
Signed love, signed with a row of Xs.

When we part from someone we might not
see again, knowing he was ill, our words
are forgotten as usual, and one can only hope
we said, "I love you," terrible if not,

and also thank you. For his kindness, for sweet
inspiration. And there's a sense of a void,
an empty space though he was far off, a state
I couldn't visit, address I never saw,
in a neighborhood, leafy, where the great
poet is no longer walking the blessed Earth.

Centers of Gold

after *Appelbaum* by Gustav Klimt

The point, after all, with canvas, brush, and paint,
isn't it to beguile the viewer's eye, to cause
this moment, these lingering minutes, of pausing?

All for what, she wonders. To gaze, then look
again, to be lifted out of the self, until one

joins what she looks at. What is it? The tree
barely distinct from what surrounds it, the trunk
slowly taking shape as a vertical skeleton, with fruit,

apples, of no variety she's known, everywhere bright
and laden, drooping at the ends of branches.

In the middle ground, a meadow where, yellow, tall,
two drifts of common dandelion sway knee high.
The foreground's a riot of cosmos: pink, white,

crimson, and burgundy, some with centers of gold.
She refuses to move from the spot, a wooden bench

where she sits alert, leaning in. There it is—
a shadow under the boughs. It had to be there,
the darkened place, ominous future of fallen

apples, also of her and her love, what she's sure
is coming and can't accept, beauty's attendant cost.

Italian Madonna

On the Ohio side, we're driving above the limit,
so the roadside weeds look like a yellow blur.

In the June sunlight, so bright I squint,
the cars around us shine metallic and hot.

Everyone we pass is in shorts, short sleeves,
shivering in A/C but soaking up sun through glass.

They seem lost in GPS fog and maps
or checking email, sending texts.

                  In the Shirley Hazzard story
the lovers walk to a farmhouse through a field

in a time that seems ancient, pre-cell phone,
pre-anything digital. Tancredi touches Sophie's

collar to straighten it—a kiss. Then she watches
his back as he walks ahead of her through poppies.

Love's an emotion she'd left out of travel.
Finding him In Italy has been a surprise.

Now they step into a cowshed to see
an old fresco high enough they need a ladder.

Sophie goes first and Tancredi holds uprights
to steady it. She doesn't fear falling.

It's too late for that. It can't end well.
There's a wife, though she's left him, and two

children waiting at home. The fresco's
moldy, in disrepair, with a dark red

background and a seated figure balancing
a child on one knee. The Madonna glows

and has a ray of corn-colored hair. This
was a monastery, long abandoned, and this

the sole object left.
                                How much better never to read,
never to imagine other lives, trying to lose oneself

in the Queen Anne's lace and grass bending
along I-69 south, then I-23 for miles.

Around us the humidity haze of summer,
sexy weather my husband sometimes calls it,

for how we longed to remove our shoes and clothes,
but never did, especially outdoors.

                                It had come
to Sophie that she'd never love Tancredi more than
on that ladder, and the thought stayed with her

as she packed her bag, folding the shirt whose
collar he had touched in a poppy field

Gold Espadrilles

I bought them at a market
in a small village in France—

across the square, items laid out
on tables—purses, hats, shoes.

A rope wedge sole and gold
fabric with a sparkly design

like a galactic spiral.
They didn't exactly fit

but good enough and cheap—
I wear them in summer

or in the fall, at evening,
when it's hot. Now I recall

I took them back to France
with me two years ago.

We walked to dinner near
the Eiffel Tower and my friend

Ann was still alive. We linked
arms, laughing, strolling—

my feet hurt, maybe her knee.
The spiral sparkled and seemed

to turn like the stars above,
sky over Paris, blue-black that night.

Elegy Not to Be Written

Can't remember now the year he died.
It might have been April. Two years ago?

I saw on Facebook he was in a coma.
I read that they might amputate his feet.

It was too much and I turned away.
Who wants all that displayed to the world?

Was it indecent of me to go walk along the river?
How I had loved him once!
Thrilled to be a bride. Some chapters

are shorter than others. I said
a prayer for his health.

At the Grand River where I walk, a place
where a black willow leans over water,

there's a patch of milkweed, stalks
and pods knocked down by deer
or random dogs, plus weather,

pods split open, soft gray,

all the fluff inside drifted off,
only a few seeds reaching the chance
of arable ground.

What My Father Wished For

I could never say anything about my father
except he was quiet, and next to Mother
he receded like a hermit crab into its shell.
Is that an excuse, at seventeen, for raising
my voice against him, trying my best
to goad him to anger? "How can you just go
to work, drive downtown, day after day,
arriving on time, leaving at five? Don't you
ever start asking yourself what it all means?"
Someone should have slapped me. I see
the kitchen at Browns Point, a round table where
we sat, high cliff light over the bay,
smoky stink of pulp mills, a madrona tree
by the deck sickened by sewage. He's about
to drive me to Stadium High, down Snake Hill,
across Tacoma's tide flats, drawbridges opening
and closing like jaws for tankers heading
out west to Japan, stacked high with lumber
or salt, later, jeeps and tanks for Vietnam.
And then I badgered him, too: "Why can't you
take a stand against the war?" This, hurled
at my father who'd enlisted after Pearl Harbor
with his favorite brother, a brother who didn't
come home from Germany. Did someone
call regret "permanent remorse"? After my father's
diagnosis, he refused to talk about death. "I've had everything
in life I could have wanted." When the priest
came to the house, Dad sat up in bed, talking
as though he'd be around weeks, as the sunset
turned salmon, then mauve over
Commencement Bay. Later, he leaned in, close
to me, to say, "One thing, though, I wish
I'd had a sister." He told me this, *sotto voce,*
when I sat alone beside him, holding his hand
through the metal rails.

Painter Joan Mitchell Pulls Me Up

What was in the air was leaf-fall, the rot
of the year's perennials and annuals, stems

and blossom ends done for, going back to earth.
I couldn't move for being caught by the suck

of quicksand, a clump of blue feathers smacked
on a window from a hit. Here I am on a cold Friday

and to my amazement the painter Joan
Mitchell reaches for me, from her oil

on canvas, a diptych called *Weeds*,
grabbing hold of me, saying "Here,

take my hand!" There's something about
her seeming riot of marks that's giving

a calming and cooling effect. It's cobalt blue,
orange, tawny, and flecked with white,

even a spot or two of sage, and I see
the trailside at Huff Park with tall

teasel, Queen Anne's lace, and a waving
frond of goldenrod or a flat-topped

white aster. Each year I'm caught watching
this awakening starting in early spring,

a mere sprout or two at first, then
climbing, growing, a stem hoisting itself up

all season till it's five feet high,
shedding petals, pollen, and seeds. Not

a riot at all, a cyclic process of
great determination, genetics, chance,

weather, sunlight, rain. Right now,
I'm bowing to the botanical display and to two

canvasses of supreme order, remembering
our visit to the Baltimore Art Museum, August,

standing in front of the actual paintings,
work as sturdy and wrought

as any palace. Then we went walking off
in a pack for lunch, having salad and Chesapeake oysters

on the half-shell along with a crisp
citrus-tasting wine. Good friends, fellow

artists, a couple more hands to pull me
out of quicksand. Where do we turn, lost

on that trail, or sinking? The Baltimore light
was pure lemon as we strolled through

the galleries pointing, talking, saying
look at that magenta, violet, sage, her vision,

her ability to make these marks. The gleam of it
lasting as long as the light, what we call a day.

My Sister's Osprey

Wrapped in a Christmas box of gifts,
the artwork in colored pen and ink surprised me,
a method I'd never seen—filling in the shape
of an osprey with Native symbols and icons,
here the head of a beaver with its two front teeth,
there the orange claw of a lobster, another showing
a mountain with snow flying, and here, larger, a vivid
dragonfly with a red thorax and green-golden wings,
the whole bird edged with gold and its wings straight up.
Just risen from the water, it gripped a rainbow trout
in its talons, the bird appearing not to struggle at all
with the weight. When I called to thank Chris,
she said she'd never seen an osprey, not knowing
it was the Egyptian symbol of the soul. I didn't say
I wondered if I was the trout, carried aloft by her,
my wounds sore. I wanted to ask if she remembered
driving with me in Seattle, years ago, in my old
blue car, on a day we saw a triple rainbow. She cried
out, in astonishment, "Oh my God, look at that!"
So many things had not yet happened to us—
meeting Dan and Art, ruptures of divorce, so many tears
long distance over the phone, talking it all through
as though betrayal could be understood like an equation.
On the news last night they showed photos from
the Hubble telescope, a woman scientist exclaiming
in tones of sheer delight about spectroscopy, how
the photos help scientists understand what happened millions
of years ago. It's similar to how we sifted through details
of our lives, never finding much. Isn't there more ahead for us,
Chris? I propose a road trip to the Chesapeake or to Maine,
perhaps, to find ospreys, so you can hear their cries, see
platform nests, how they hunt, and learn how fierce they are
to defend what's theirs. I want to be back together with you
in a car, near an overlook or a saltwater beach, seeing something
miraculous, and living to tell the tale

Our Next Breath

My husband's talking through the music on the radio,
some melodic jazz I don't know, and telling all
about the bassist, how some years after
the record was made, he was diagnosed with bipolar
disease, from then on his life hit the skids, down
and down, homeless in D.C., addiction and more,
halfway houses and treatments that never worked.

Then one of the other players, a trumpet legend,
was shot by his jealous girlfriend at a nightclub
called Slugs in NY City. The stories bleed from one
to the next, while the sax, the trumpet, double bass,
the drums keep the beat and I'm unconsciously toe-tapping,
trying to listen. By the time the deejay comes back
on, Stan says all of the players are dead,

none left to hear this today, hear their own names,
or collect the royalties they are surely due.
Sometimes the injustices stack up so high, tilting,
they could topple and crash. Over ten days, there's a war
in Ukraine, started by Russia for no good reason.
A million refugees trying to get out, find a place
to sleep, and stories on the news of people
scrambling to get on trains for Poland.

We turn off the news because it's terrifying,
and there's nothing we can do, but the next day
it's the zoo at Kyiv that makes me cry—
fifty people have moved in with their families,
God knows how, to console the old Asian elephant
and calm the wolves, to cuddle the baby lemur
abandoned by its shellshocked mama, and give food
and water so all the animals can survive.

The other night I said we can't give up joy.
Our friend David had to put his cat Leo
to sleep but plans for a new cat very soon.

I bend to allium bulbs tucked in the ground
last fall, soon to be pulled up by the sun and spring
rains. Next to our walkway, a clump of scilla—
a startling blue. Going on as we can, looking up
and out, uncertain as our next breath.

You Can't Have Everything You Want

But you can have votives, unscented and white,
enough to light one every day just the same way
you peel the clementine. You can have sweet
ones, discarding the sour. You can have the dog,
tricolored, rescued, the one who needs pills
to stay calm, but who doesn't? You can have,
in October, all the golden trees—mainly ash
and oak. You can keep on learning French,
each day lessons with a focus on home or work,
art or sport, and you can dream of speaking it
in France though that may be a bit of a stretch.
You can try Paris again, this time choosing
the best arrondissement, one near museums.
But you can't bring your friend back, the one
who walked there. Remember the Pompidou
and the salty oysters at lunch? She can't
answer. Try somebody else. You can
be grateful for birds, even ones you can't see:
today the Savannah sparrow, American pipit,
the pipit common on tundra—why would it be here?
You can celebrate the man with the painterly eye
who helps you pick out plants—this purple
ornamental cabbage and what color mums?
Choose the russet, the barely opened, the still-
to-be-beautiful. And pansies—white, purple, blue,
and gold. You'll tuck them into a window box.
You can't ensure they'll live past a hard frost,
but no one can. You can cover them with plastic
for the night; you can tuck in clumps of straw.
Sometimes you can't fill the house with people
the way you wanted, though you remember a night
of snow, a birthday in December, cake and ice cream
on dessert plates garlanded with flowers and bees.
A memory's almost as good as having friends here
again, the windows steaming up, champagne
chilled and about to pop, cars ticking as they cool
in the driveway, everyone's footsteps filling with white.

Hokusai's Views of Mt. Fuji

Do you want me to count them?
In this book, there are twenty-four.

Framed by an ocean wave,
behind a fleet of small fishing boats.

Almost hidden by a terrace garden,
a man laboring with water in a bucket.

In a winter cabin, people gather at the window
to point at the peak, three soaring birds.

Here a summer scene, the white slope
gone to dry burnishment, almost golden.

Circle and the peak, a man hammering
slats of a large cask, then sealing it with tar.

Only two views of the mountain alone,
no human, no sign of a hut, boat, bridge.

The peak tall, cliffs ridged and stark,
clouds drift below like lily pads on a pond.

Döstädning: Beginner's Translation

Some words arrive with little music, some bring
three difficult syllables that sound rough
to your ears. Still, you repeat them, not
your language, sounding them out, trying
to wet syllables with your tongue and mouth,
adding moisture, and maybe they'll dance
or at least roll around. *Dust* is what you hear
first, and it's ashes to ashes, dust to dust
lifting in a swirl, Ash Wednesday mornings
when the priest thumbed your forehead
with a cross, one you wore all day, silly pride
of elementary school belonging—*my tribe.*
Then *ad*, now you're adding the scene where
you opened the flowered box from the pet
crematorium—gray stuff with flecks of white, bits
smaller than mustard seeds that could be bone.
What sorcery is this? Molly the Aussie dog
who ran and leaped, now inert particles, clay
that could be modelled into a fine bowl. Standing
in the vet office, you didn't understand when
the clerk asked, "Group or individual ashes?"
Ning is the stuff of it, thingy tangibles of life:
hats, purses, shoes, bracelets and rings,
necklaces, books, boxes in the basement stuffed
with photos and notebooks, all the clothes that hang
in your closet, ghosts of who you were
once upon a time—in front of a class, or saying words
at a podium and mic, wearing a red silk
jacket. Reversible, other side black. Life, time,
both visualized as sand sifting through a funnel, narrowing down
to a point somewhere ahead. How long yet do I have?
The Swedish, a practical breed with economy
on their minds, believe in a clean cupboard like
a conscience. Well ahead of your own demise, death-
cleaning they call it. Go ahead, open your closet,
and pick up a red shoe.

I Like How They Gather

in spring, the big crows. I'm seeing three
       right now, high up, raucous in an old
battered oak. They don't take shit

from anyone—blue jays or red-tailed hawks.

In a survey I saw about coming back, next
       life and all, experts offered a celebrity life,
even a princess or two. I'd rather

slit my throat. Imagine the polite talk,
dress codes, afternoon teas, along with self-

censoring of thoughts and words. I'd be a crow,
       a red fox, I'd even be an early peeper,
pseudacris triseriata, or a plump woodchuck

instead. I saw one by our neighbor's green shed
take a couple of bites out of a month-old

deer carcass. There's a word for that—
       omnivore. Compared to a princess
with allergies, gluten-free diet, even lactose

intolerance, I'd be that groundhog. Fat.

My Mother's Shoes

are not as beautiful as I'd like them to be:
     they are white, thick-soled,

she limps in them, and another pair, sandals,
     reveal her gnarled toes under wide

Velcro straps. I go back in time, her closet,
     seeking ones I can put on a pedestal,

heels of an ice blue for a wedding, perhaps,
     narrow shoes with an instep arch

curved sexy as a woman's waist or like
     the graceful line of neck into

collar—clavicle, bone, our link to birds
     and flight, always the swan.

Now I see her walking barefoot down
     to Commencement Bay, and the islands

out across the water are blue-green hulks
     that could be whales.

Her sister, Ruth, is visiting from Rowley—
     what year is this? Back

from the dead, they are the age I am now,
     no longer young, and I hardly

notice my mother's leg veins, purple
     and knotted, or Ruth's belly protruding.

They bend together in laughter, holding
     hands. It's all sand, no

shoes needed and they walk in beauty
     into the forgiving hem of water,

up to their ankles, knees, and thighs. Then, free
     of gravity, they splash in and swim.

Blooms Gripped in a Fist

A child's voice in a documentary long ago,
the narrator asking, as he'll ask multiple
kids, "What's it like to be old?"

This boy sits in a small chair, kicking his heels
against the chair leg. Dark hair, dark
eyes that have witnessed. "It's loose skin."

Others offer different answers like a bunch
of blooms gripped in a fist—black-eyed Susans,
bluebells and delphinium, liatris, daffs.

"It's when you forget a lot." A girl, softly,
"You walk more slowly." Redheaded boy, "You've lived
through many wars and many times." I look down

at my arm, how the skin on the lower part
of my right bicep is wrinkled and ruckled
like the sand along a shore, water gone.

Do I drink my eight to ten glasses a day?
At the park, along the river, I keep up my pace
with a dog—our third one. I know years,

presidents, and wars. Some of our friends, all
of our parents, are no longer walking the Earth.
What is it to be old? Another says, cloudy eyes.

The children do not seem afraid. This one says
how his grandmother taught him to thread a needle,
"It's fun to sew a button on a shirt!"

They make a few distinctions between what's seen
and what's not. A bent back, loose skin, gray
hair, but "My grandfather groans when he stands up."

To rise each day, the living, and breathing, urge.
The children have said enough; now they dance away,
out of the studio into the bright air.

Elegy to Be Breathed at the Grand River

Choose a fall night. Choose October's last night
when the costumed children go door-to-door, scaring

only themselves. Remember the year a little girl
cried at our door, saying, "I didn't want to be a bride"?

The girl turned and flounced away while her mother
laughed. This elegy is for the girl. If you choose

a good night, the ground will exhale along
with the river, a shimmer of leafshine, russet,

maroon, amber, scarlet. Notice how those
colors ripple in the water, inviting you in.

No one swims in the river, but fishermen
wade out there to the middle, avoiding

sudden holes, hitching up hip boots, sliding
felted boots along, feeling for stones.

Elements of sorrow and goodbye are fitting
for elegy. I'm going nowhere but home,

holding the little girl's hand, trying to tell
her I could be her mother. It's not going

to work. The sass between them is bond
and DNA. When I spit in the tube, mailed

it in, my cousins proliferated like fruit
flies. Who are they all? The family lines

tangled like mistaken birdsong—
is that a great horned owl or a boy

hoo-hooing for an echo? A kingfisher
or a maraca being shaken at the nearby

Mexican restaurant? This elegy features
refreshments—ghost food and sweets

for the journey. White cauliflower steamed
and dipped in melted cheese, mashed

potatoes and milk, a trout amandine covered
in cream. Chocolate mousse in ramekins

and an almond tart to end with. Take your
sweet time. Let's wash it down with wine,

as purple as dusk coming on, or as the bruise
the girl's wrist shows, from her mother's grip.

36 Myopia Road

for the house where I might have grown up, in Winchester, MA

I cannot see past the houses lining
this street. Next door is 34
and across the street are odd
numbers. Overhead, pelicans fly
in search of seawater and fish,
or do I mean chimneys and storks?

An hour to Marblehead Lighthouse.
A house on the corner with a wide porch
finally sold. I imagined our family there
in future years. A red-headed girl named Ruth
never went to school. Always playing hopscotch.
I think of her as one-legged and blind.

A few houses wore rumors floating in air
around them. Someone said a cardboard box
of puppies had been buried alive.
A boy heard them whimpering all night
under fir trees that sighed. Next day
there wasn't a sign or any proof.

When my people left for the West Coast, an egg
in my mother's belly started to grow
into me. I can see the family sleeping
in fields as they crossed North and South
Dakota. Ripe apricots filched from trees,
field corn to break teeth on. Tomatoes, cukes.

Settling into the Puget Sound's salt air,
they awaited my birth like the Messiah.
Stars aligned and Magi came on horse-
and camel-back. Once, a blue and white
parakeet appeared in a pine tree. My mother
tried to catch it and then I was born.

I was afraid of deadly nightshade berries. *atropa belladonna*, plump in the bushes in a border near our house. Pretending to eat them, we'd gag, falling dead. We played rock school on the porch steps, banishing the witch, kickball in the street. Dusk coming down always made it look like home.

In Which I Consider Intimacy While Making Paella

Today's recipe—arborio rice to be toasted on a sheet
pan, oven set high, then broth added, more
heat. Of course, the seasoning goes in,
saffron, bay leaf, paprika, pepper, and salt.

If separate beds are to intimacy a closed
door, then a new way of making love
is the method of lying down together,
in peace, syncing our breathing afterwards.

Cover the pan, don't forget. Only later,
piling on top: mussels, shrimp with tails,
thin slices of chorizo. Is your mouth

watering yet? In both cases, do you see what
anticipation adds? Ending the day together.

Do you see a sexy gleam on discarded black shells?

Aphrodisiacal

Open me like an oyster. Yes, it involves
a knife and some risk. Take your time,
love, and wear a protective mitt.
Admire all my shades of gray and black.
Drink the juices from my shell, savoring
the salinity. Swallow any bits of grit
or shell, not worrying they will harm you.
Use a fork and dip me whole into pale
mignonette sauce. How I love its acid
notes—red wine vinegar, black pepper, minced
shallots. When I found that recipe,
I wanted oysters every week. To your
credit, you indulged me. Isn't that
the best marriage? Indulge me again,
ever so slowly. Use your mouth, your
flexible tongue. Once you've warmed me,
juices rising, anything becomes possible.
Notice how we go out of the world together,
riding a wave of flesh, warmth, holy
waters that our bodies create as one.
Discover all the openings that do not usually
gap so wide. There is nowhere else
we need to be. Bow at the altar of our
commingling. Do this again and again,
in the name of all the seas we come from.

Home Astronomy

When we came back together to sleep
in the lavender room, same bed,
there was a subtle realignment of the stars,

> planets, Milky Way. If you remain still,
> you'll hear the whole house shift and sigh,
> walls and doors, windows, window screens, chest

the dog lies beside at the foot of the bed. If we
were bricks, now mortar is in place, hardening.
Don't we use celestial bodies to navigate

> our world? Somehow we used to. Then clouds
> rolled in, obscuring them, and we couldn't see
> to see. In college, I built a telescope from foil,

cardboard tubes, tape, and glue. Did it work?
See us in sleep? My hand steers from his hip.

When the Goldfinches Return to the Purple Coneflower, He Calls to Me

They ride the blossoms, stalk-swaying,
      fluttering to keep their balance,
and I notice it's the female pulling out
      a thistle from the flower center,
eating it, then digging for another.

Sometimes he says we don't talk enough,
      or that he can't get a word in
when we go out with friends. At Licari's,
      over Italian food, he said the servers
always came over, too, and interrupted him.

Sometimes I wonder who will go first,
      which one of us, I mean, feeling a clutch
at my heart. Resolve—talk more, listen
      better. Then he calls me to look
and we stand side by side, united, as one.

We watch the goldfinches together, right out
      the dining room window, first four,
then six of them with black and white wing bars,
      their black foreheads. Then in a whisk,
they go straight out to the woods.

Acknowledgments

Many thanks to the editors of the following journals who first published these poems, sometimes with a different title or in a slightly altered version.

Alaska Quarterly Review: "When the Goldfinches Return to the Purple Coneflowers, He Calls to Me"

Atticus Review: "Juneberry Leaves as Gold Coins"

Cimarron Review: "Hokusai's Views of Mt. Fuji," "In Which I Consider Intimacy While Making Paella"

EcoTheo Review: "Forest Bathing"

Galway Review: "Our Next Breath," "Portrait of My Lover as a Promenade Along the Sea"

I-70 Review: "Home Astronomy"

The Midwest Quarterly: "Elegy Not to Be Written," "Fathering," "The Wind Phone"

North American Review: "Give Me a Face"

Pedestal: "Elegy to Be Breathed at the Grand River"

Pensive: "Silver-Tipped Japanese Grass"

Pleiades: "I Like How They Gather"

Plume: "Aphrodisiacal," "Because What We Do Lives On," "Centers of Gold," "Döstädning: Beginner's Translation," "Love Poem to a Red Fox," "Oxygen," "Passing Royalty," "What My Father Wished For"

The Polaris Trilogy: Poems for the Moon: "Astronomy 'In Perfect Silence,'" Ed. Joyce Brinkman et al, Brick Street Poetry, Inc., 2023

Quartet: "Blooms Gripped in a Fist"

Salt: "I Consider Pruning the Magnolia and Instead Take a Nap," "Sea Urchin" as "Barnacle"

Sheila-Na-Gig: "36 Myopia Road"

The Southern Review: "You Can't Have Everything You Want"

Superstition Review: "Char"

TAB: A Journal of Poetry & Poetics: "Poem Beginning with a Line from Adam Zagajewski"

Tar River Poetry: "After My Husband Tries His New Electric Shaver"

Third Coast: "Each Day I Undress"

UCity Review: "Inscape, with Birdsong," "Italian Madonna," "Soldier Boy," "When the Great Poet Is Gone from the Earth"

upstreet: "My Mother's Shoes"

Valparaiso Review: "Gold Espadrilles," "Quarentena"

Westchester Review: "Sailor"

Thanks to Joyce Brinkman for the invitation to write "Astronomy: 'In Perfect Silence'" for the Lunar Codex project.

Many thanks to my teachers, especially Nelson Bentley, Richard Hugo, Madeline DeFrees, Naomi Lazard, Stanley Plumly, Cythia Macdonald, and Edward Hirsch.

Thanks to my colleagues and students at Grand Valley State University for many years of lively conversations and writing from which I learned so much.

Thanks to poets Alice Fulton, Alice Friman, Richard Robbins, and M.L. Liebler for reading my poems and also manuscript drafts that were greatly improved by your acuity. Thanks to David Baker, Naomi Shihab Nye, and M.L. Liebler for your thoughtful endorsements. Thanks to many other poets too numerous to name whose work stimulated me and opened doors in my imagination to new ideas about poetry.

Thanks to Zoom poets/friends Rasma Haidri, Paula Finn, and Luci Huhn for monthly meetings, great conversations, and wonderful critiques. Thanks to poet Ellen Bass and her *Living Room Craft Talks* and the Zoom group who continued to meet afterward: thanks to you all!

Thanks to Linda Parsons and Kim Davis at Madville Publishing for your encouragement, enthusiasm, and for the beautiful books you make.

Lastly, to Stan Krohmer, for his steady encouragement, support, and love. Thanks for your paintings!

About the Author

Patricia Clark is the author of six volumes of poetry, including *Sunday Rising*, *The Canopy*, and most recently *Self-Portrait with a Million Dollars*. Her work has appeared in *The Atlantic*, *Gettysburg Review*, *Poetry*, and *Slate*, among others. Awards include a Creative Artist Grant in Michigan, the Mississippi Review Prize, the Gwendolyn Brooks Prize, and co-winner of the Lucille Medwick Prize from the Poetry Society of America. She also received the 2018 Book of the Year Award from the Poetry Society of Virginia for *The Canopy*. Clark was professor in the Department of Writing at Grand Valley State University, where she was the university's poet-in-residence. She was also poet laureate of the city of Grand Rapids from 2005-2007. Her poem "Astronomy 'In Perfect Silence'" was chosen to go to the moon on the NASA/ Space X launch in November 2024 as part of the Lunar Codex.